Congressional
Research Service
Informing the legislative debate since 1914 _____

# Navy Irregular Warfare and Counterterrorism Operations: Background and Issues for Congress

Ronald O'Rourke
Specialist in Naval Affairs

June 25, 2014

Congressional Research Service

7-5700

www.crs.gov

RS22373

# Summary

The Navy for several years has carried out a variety of irregular warfare (IW) and counterterrorism (CT) activities. Among the most readily visible of the Navy's recent IW operations have been those carried out by Navy sailors serving ashore in Afghanistan and Iraq. Many of the Navy's contributions to IW operations around the world are made by Navy individual augmentees (IAs)—individual Navy sailors assigned to various Department of Defense (DOD) operations.

The May 1-2, 2011, U.S. military operation in Abbottabad, Pakistan, that killed Osama bin Laden reportedly was carried out by a team of 23 Navy special operations forces, known as SEALs (an acronym standing for Sea, Air, and Land). The SEALs reportedly belonged to an elite unit known unofficially as Seal Team 6 and officially as the Naval Special Warfare Development Group (DEVGRU).

The Navy established the Navy Expeditionary Combat Command (NECC) informally in October 2005 and formally in January 2006. NECC consolidated and facilitated the expansion of a number of Navy organizations that have a role in IW operations. The Navy established the Navy Irregular Warfare Office in July 2008, published a vision statement for irregular warfare in January 2010, and established "a community of interest" to develop and advance ideas, collaboration, and advocacy related to IW in December 2010.

The Navy's riverine force is intended to supplement the riverine capabilities of the Navy's SEALs and relieve Marines who had been conducting maritime security operations in ports and waterways in Iraq.

The Global Maritime Partnership is a U.S. Navy initiative to achieve an enhanced degree of cooperation between the U.S. Navy and foreign navies, coast guards, and maritime police forces, for the purpose of ensuring global maritime security against common threats.

The Southern Partnership Station (SPS) and the Africa Partnership Station (APS) are Navy ships, such as amphibious ships or high-speed sealift ships, that have deployed to the Caribbean and to waters off Africa, respectively, to support U.S. Navy engagement with countries in those regions, particularly for purposes of building security partnerships with those countries and for increasing the capabilities of those countries for performing maritime-security operations.

The Navy's IW and CT activities pose a number of potential oversight issues for Congress, including how much emphasis to place on IW and CT activities in future Navy budgets.

# Contents

# Appendixes

# Contacts

# Introduction

This report provides background information and potential issues for Congress on the Navy's irregular warfare (IW) and counterterrorism (CT) operations. The Navy's IW and CT activities pose a number of potential oversight issues for Congress, including how much emphasis to place on IW and CT activities in future Navy budgets. Congress's decisions regarding Navy IW and CT operations can affect Navy operations and funding requirements, and the implementation of the nation's overall IW and CT strategies.

# Background

## Navy Irregular Warfare (IW) Operations

### Note on Terminology

The Department of Defense's (DOD's) report on the 2014 Quadrennial Defense Review (QDR), like DOD's report on the 2010 QDR, avoids the term irregular warfare and instead uses terms such as counterinsurgency and stability operations. The Navy sometimes uses the phrase confronting irregular challenges (CIC) instead of the term irregular warfare. For purposes of convenience, this report continues to use the term irregular warfare and the abbreviation IW.

### Navy IW Operations in Afghanistan and Iraq

Among the most readily visible of the Navy's IW (and CT) operations in recent years have been those carried out by Navy sailors serving ashore in Afghanistan and (in earlier years) Iraq. Regarding its operations in the Middle East, the Department of the Navy (DON) states the following in its FY2015 budget highlights book:

> FY 2014 continues supporting Navy and Marine Corps operations in Afghanistan. Today the Marine Corps has a declining force of ~8,000 Marines in the U.S. Central Command (CENTCOM) with 3,900 in Afghanistan, reflecting the continuing responsible drawdown of forces in Afghanistan.
>
> Beyond the Marines participating in counterinsurgency, security cooperation, and civil-military operations in Afghanistan and throughout CENTCOM, on any given day there are approximately 6,000 Sailors ashore and another 10,000 afloat throughout CENTCOM. These Sailors are conducting, maritime infrastructure protection, explosive ordnance disposal/(Counter-IED), combat construction engineering, cargo handling, combat logistics, maritime security, customs inspections, detainee operations, civil affairs, base operations and other forward presence activities. In collaboration with the U.S. Coast Guard, the Navy also conducts critical port operations and maritime interception operations. Included in our globally sourced forces are Individual Augmentees (IAs) serving in a variety of joint or coalition billets, either in the training pipeline or on station. As these operations unfold, the size and type of naval forces committed to them will likely evolve, thereby producing changes to the overall posture of naval forces. For the foreseeable future, the demand for naval presence in the theater remains high as we uphold our commitments to allies and partner states. The maintenance of peace, stability, the free flow of commerce, and U.S. interests in this dynamic region will depend on naval presence and the ability to strike

violent extremist groups when necessary. Long after the significant land component of the operation is reduced, naval forces will remain forward.[1]

DON also states that the

> versatility and lethality [of U.S. naval forces] can be applied across the spectrum of operations, from destroying terrorist base camps and protecting friendly forces involved in sustained counterinsurgency or stability operations, to defeating enemy anti-access defenses in support of amphibious operations. We have focused this strategic capability intensely in Afghanistan in an effort to counter the increasing threat of a well-armed anti-Coalition militia including Taliban, al-Qa'ida, criminal gangs, narco-terrorists, and any other antigovernment elements that threaten the peace and stability of Afghanistan. Our efforts to deter or defeat aggression and improve overall security and counter violent extremism and terrorist networks advance the interests of the U.S. and the security of the region.[2]

DON also states that

> The Navy's RC [reserve component] fulfills the preponderance of the Department's adversary and intratheater logistics requirements. The Navy RC helicopter footprint in the CENTCOM Area of Responsibility has been continuous since 2003, supporting special operations ground-force missions, psychological operations, and medical and casualty evacuations.[3]

## Navy IW Operations Elsewhere

In addition to participating in U.S. military operations in Afghanistan and Iraq, the Navy IW operations also include the following:

- **security force assistance operations**, in which forward-deployed Navy ships exercise and work with foreign navies, coast guards, and maritime police forces, so as to improve their abilities to conduct maritime security operations;

- **civic assistance operations**, in which forward-deployed Navy units, including Navy hospital ships, expeditionary medical teams, fleet surgical teams, and naval construction units provide medical and construction services in foreign countries as a complement to other U.S. diplomatic and development activities in those countries;

- **disaster relief operations**, of which Navy forces have performed several in recent years; and

- **counter-piracy operations**.[4]

---

[1] Department of the Navy, *Highlights of the Department of the Navy FY 2015 Budget*, 2014, pp. 7-1 and 7-2.

[2] Department of the Navy, *Highlights of the Department of the Navy FY 2015 Budget*, 2014, pp. 7-2 and 7-3.

[3] Department of the Navy, *Highlights of the Department of the Navy FY 2015 Budget*, 2014, p. 3-18.

[4] For more on counter-piracy operations, see CRS Report R40528, *Piracy off the Horn of Africa*, by Lauren Ploch Blanchard et al.

## Navy Individual Augmentees (IAs)

Many of the Navy's contributions to IW operations around the world are made by Navy individual augmentees (IAs)—individual Navy sailors assigned to various DOD operations. DON states that:

> Navy IAs are providing combat support and combat service support for Army and Marine Corps personnel in Afghanistan. As IAs they are fulfilling vital roles by serving in traditional Navy roles such as USMC support, maritime and port security, cargo handling, airlift support, Seabee units, and as a member of joint task force/Combatant Commanders staffs. Non-traditional roles include detainee operations, custom inspections teams, and civil affairs.[5]

## November 2011 Navy Testimony

The Navy outlined its IW activities in its prepared statement for a November 3, 2011, hearing on the services' IW activities before the Emerging Threats and Capabilities subcommittee of the House Armed Services Committee. For the text of the Navy's prepared statement, see **Appendix A**.

## 2012 RAND Corporation Report

A 2012 report on maritime irregular warfare from RAND Corporation, a research firm, provides additional background information on U.S. maritime irregular warfare operations, both recent and historical.[6] The report also made a series of findings and recommendations relating to U.S. maritime irregular warfare; for a summary of these findings and recommendations, see **Appendix B**.

# Navy Counterterrorism (CT) Operations

## In General

Navy CT operations include the following:

- Operations by Navy special operations forces, known as SEALs (an acronym standing for Sea, Air, and Land), that are directed against terrorists;[7]

- Tomahawk cruise missile attacks on suspected terrorist training camps and facilities, such as those reportedly conducted in Somalia on March 3 and May 1, 2008,[8] and those conducted in 1998 in response to the 1998 terrorist bombings of U.S. embassies in East Africa;[9]

---

[5] Department of the Navy, *Highlights of the Department of the Navy FY 2015 Budget*, 2014, p. 7-3.

[6] Molly Dunigan, et al, *Characterizing and Exploring the Implications of Maritime Irregular Warfare*, RAND Corporation, Santa Monica (CA), 2012, 111 p.

[7] For an account of a series of missions reportedly conducted by SEALS over a six-week period in November and December 2003 to plant cameras in Somalia for the purpose of conducting surveillance on terrorists, see Sean D. Naylor, "Hunting Down Terrorists," *Army Times*, November 7, 2011: 22.

[8] Edmund Sanders, "U.S. Missile Strike in Somalia Kills 6," *Los Angeles Times*, March 4, 2008; Stephanie (continued...)

---

- surveillance by Navy ships and aircraft of suspected terrorists overseas;

- maritime intercept operations (MIO) aimed at identifying and intercepting terrorists or weapons of mass destruction at sea, or potentially threatening ships or aircraft that are in or approaching U.S. territorial waters—an activity that includes Navy participation in the multilateral Proliferation Security Initiative (PSI);[10]

- protection of forward-deployed Navy ships, an activity that was intensified following the terrorist attack on the Navy Aegis destroyer *Cole* (DDG-67) in October 2000 in the port of Aden, Yemen;[11]

- protection of domestic and overseas Navy bases and facilities;

- working with the Coast Guard to build maritime domain awareness (or MDA, meaning a real-time understanding of activities on the world's oceans), and engaging with the U.S. Coast Guard to use the National Strategy for Maritime Security to more rapidly develop capabilities for Homeland Security, particularly in the area of MDA;

- assisting the Coast Guard in port-security operations;[12]

- developing Global Maritime Intelligence Integration (GMII) as part of Joint Force Maritime Component Command (JFMCC) and Maritime Domain Awareness (MDA); and

- operations by the Naval Criminal Investigative Service (NCIS), for which combating terrorism is a core mission area.[13]

---

(...continued)

McCrummen and Karen DeYoung, "U.S. Airstrike Kills Somali Accused of Links to Al-Qaeda," *Washington Post*, May 2, 2008: A12; Eric Schmitt and Jeffrey Gettleman, "Qaeda Leader Reported Killed In Somalia," *New York Times*, May 2, 2008.

[9] For an article on the 1998 strikes, see Pamela Hess, "Report: 1998 Strike Built bin Laden-Taliban Tie," *NavyTimes.com (Associated Press)*, August 22, 2008.

[10] For more on the PSI, see CRS Report RL34327, *Proliferation Security Initiative (PSI)*, by Mary Beth D. Nikitin.

[11] For a discussion of the attack on the Cole, see CRS Report RS20721, *Terrorist Attack on USS Cole: Background and Issues for Congress*, by Raphael F. Perl and Ronald O'Rourke.

[12] See, for example, Emelie Rutherford, "Navy's Maritime Domain Awareness System 'Up And Running'," *Defense Daily*, September 4, 2008; and Dan Taylor, "New Network Allows Navy To Track Thousands of Ships Worldwide," *Inside the Navy*, September 8, 2008. For more on the Coast Guard and port security, see CRS Report RL33383, *Terminal Operators and Their Role in U.S. Port and Maritime Security*, by John Frittelli and Jennifer E. Lake, and CRS Report RL33787, *Maritime Security: Potential Terrorist Attacks and Protection Priorities*, by Paul W. Parfomak and John Frittelli.

[13] NCIS states on its website that "the NCIS mission is to investigate and defeat criminal, foreign, and terrorist intelligence threats to the United States Navy and Marine Corps, wherever they operate: ashore, afloat, or in cyberspace," and that combating terrorism is a core mission area for NCIS. Regarding this mission, the website states that

> Protecting the naval forces from violent extremist organizations and individuals is one of NCIS' highest priorities. As the primary law enforcement and counterintelligence component for the naval services, NCIS is focused on countering threats to the physical security of Sailors, Marines, and Department of the Navy (DON) civilian personnel and on preventing terrorist attacks against installations and ships.

> NCIS is responsible for detecting, deterring, and disrupting terrorism worldwide through a wide array of offensive and defensive capabilities. Offensive operations aim at identifying and

(continued...)

DON states that

> While forward, acting as the lead element of our defense-in-depth, naval forces will be positioned for increased roles in combating terrorism.... Expanded Maritime Interdiction Operations are authorized by the President and directed by the Secretary of Defense to intercept vessels identified to be transporting terrorists and/or terrorist-related materiel that poses an imminent threat to the United States and its allies.....
>
> We have done small, precise attacks against terrorist cells and missile attacks against extremist sanctuaries.[14]

DON also states that

> Our defense efforts are aimed at countering violent extremists and destabilizing threats, as well as upholding our commitments to allies and partner states. These armed adversaries such as terrorists, insurgents, and separatist militias are a principal challenge to U.S. interests in East Africa.[15]

An April 8, 2013, press report about U.S. counter-terrorism operations stated, regarding one particular operation, that

> The uncertainties were evident nine months into Mr. Obama's first term, when intelligence agencies tracked down Saleh Ali Saleh Nabhan, a suspect in the attacks on two American embassies in East Africa in 1998.
>
> The original plan had been to fire long-range missiles to hit Mr. Nabhan and others as they drove in a convoy from Mogadishu, Somalia, to the seaside town of Baraawe. But that plan was scrubbed at the last minute, and instead a Navy SEALs[16] team helicopter from a ship and strafed Mr. Nabhan's convoy, killing him and three others. The SEALs landed to collect DNA samples to confirm the identities of the dead.[17]

## May 1-2, 2011, U.S. Military Operation That Killed Osama Bin Laden

The May 1-2, 2011, U.S. military operation in Abbottabad, Pakistan, that killed Osama bin Laden—reportedly called Operation Neptune's Spear—reportedly was carried out by a team of 23 Navy special operations forces, known as SEALs (an acronym standing for Sea, Air, and Land). The SEALs reportedly belonged to an elite unit known unofficially as Seal Team 6 and officially as the Naval Special Warfare Development Group (DEVGRU). The SEALs reportedly were flown to and from Abbottabad by Army special operations helicopters. Bin Laden's body reportedly was flown by a U.S. military helicopter from Abbottabad to a base in Afghanistan, and

---

(...continued)

> interdicting terrorist activities. In defensive operations, NCIS supports key DON leaders with protective services and performs physical security assessments of military installations and related facilities—including ports, airfields, and exercise areas to which naval expeditionary forces deploy.
>
> (Source: http://www ncis navy mil/CoreMissions/CT/Pages/default.aspx, accessed on November 29, 2011.)

[14] Department of the Navy, *Highlights of the Department of the Navy FY 2015 Budget*, 2014, p. 7-2.

[15] Department of the Navy, *Highlights of the Department of the Navy FY 2015 Budget*, 2013, p. 7-4.

[16] The Navy's special operations forces are known as SEALs; SEAL is an acronym that stands for Sea, Air, and Land.

[17] Scott Shane, "Targeted Killing Comes To Define War On Terror," *New York Times*, April 8, 2013: 1.

from there by a Marine Corps V-22 tilt-rotor aircraft to the aircraft carrier *Carl Vinson* (CVN-70), which was operating at the time in the Northern Arabian Sea. A few hours later, bin Laden's body reportedly was buried at sea from the ship. Differing accounts have been published regarding certain details of the operation.[18]

Press reports in July 2010 stated that U.S. forces in Afghanistan included at that time a special unit called Task Force 373, composed of Navy SEALS and Army Delta Force personnel, whose mission is "the deactivation of top Taliban and terrorists by either killing or capturing them."[19]

Another CRS report provides additional background information on the SEALs,[20] and another provides further discussion of the operation that killed Osama bin Laden.[21]

## Detention of Terrorist Suspects on Navy Ships

On July 6, 2011, it was reported that

> The U.S. military captured a Somali terrorism suspect [named Ahmed Abdulkadir Warsame] in the Gulf of Aden in April and interrogated him for more than two months aboard a U.S. Navy ship before flying him this week to New York, where he has been indicted on federal charges....
>
> Other U.S. officials, interviewed separately, said Warsame and another individual were apprehended aboard a boat traveling from Yemen to Somalia by the U.S. military's Joint Operations Command. The vessel was targeted because the United States had acquired intelligence that potentially significant operatives were on board, the officials said. Court documents said the capture took place April 19.
>
> One of the senior administration officials who briefed reporters said that the other suspect was released "after a very short period of time" after the military "determined that Warsame was an individual that we were very much interested in for further interrogation."
>
> According to court documents, Warsame was interrogated on "all but a daily basis" by military and civilian intelligence interrogators. During that time, officials in Washington held a number of meetings to discuss the intelligence being gleaned, Warsame's status and what to do with him.

---

[18] See, for example, Nicholas Schmidle, "Getting Bin Laden," *The New Yorker*, August 8, 2011, accessed online August 10, 2011 at http://www.newyorker.com/reporting/2011/08/08/110808fa_fact_schmidle; Peter Bergen, "The Last Days Of Osama Bin Laden," *Time*, May 7, 2012; Mark Bowden, "The Hunt For 'Geronimo,'" *Vanity Fair*, November 2012: 144; Chuck Pfarrer, *SEAL Target Geronimo: The Inside Story of the Mission to Kill Osama bin Laden* (St. Martin's Press, 2011), 240 pp.; Mark Owen (pseudonym) and Kevin Maurer, *No Easy Day: The Firsthand Account of the Mission That Killed Osama Bin Laden* (Dutton Adult, 2012), 336 pp.; Peter Bergen, "Who Really Killed Bin Laden," *CNN.com*, March 26, 2013.

[19] Matthias, et al, "US Elite Unit Could Create Political Fallout For Berlin," *Spiegel (Germany)*, July 26, 2010. See also C. J. Chivers, et al, "Inside the Fog Of War: Reports From The Ground In Afghanistan," *New York Times*, July 26, 2010: 1.

[20] CRS Report RS21048, *U.S. Special Operations Forces (SOF): Background and Issues for Congress*, by Andrew Feickert.

[21] CRS Report R41809, *Osama bin Laden's Death: Implications and Considerations*, coordinated by John W. Rollins.

---

The options, one official said, were to release him, transfer him to a third country, keep him prisoner aboard the ship, subject him to trial by a military commission or allow a federal court to try him. The decision to seek a federal indictment, this official said, was unanimous.

Administration officials have argued that military commission jurisdiction is too narrow for some terrorism cases - particularly for a charge of material support for terrorist groups - and the Warsame case appeared to provide an opportunity to try to prove the point.

But some human rights and international law experts criticized what they saw as at least a partial return to the discredited "black site" prisons the CIA maintained during the Bush administration....

Warsame was questioned aboard the ship because interrogators "believed that moving him to another facility would interrupt the process and risk ending the intelligence flow," one senior administration official said.

The official said Warsame "at all times was treated in a manner consistent with all Department of Defense policies" - following the Army Field Manual - and the Geneva Conventions.

Warsame was not provided access to an attorney during the initial two months of questioning, officials said. But "thereafter, there was a substantial break from any questioning of the defendant of four days," court documents said. "After this break, the defendant was advised of his Miranda rights" - including his right to legal representation – "and, after waiving those rights, spoke to law enforcement agents."

The four-day break and separate questioning were designed to avoid tainting the court case with information gleaned through un-Mirandized intelligence interrogation, an overlap that has posed a problem in previous cases. The questioning continued for seven days, "and the defendant waived his Miranda rights at the start of each day," the documents said....

U.S. Navy Vice Adm. William H. McRaven alluded to the captures in testimony before a Senate committee last week in which he lamented the lack of clear plans and legal approvals for the handling of terrorism suspects seized beyond the war zones of Iraq and Afghanistan.

At one point in the hearing, Sen. Carl Levin (D-Mich.), the chairman of the Senate Armed Services Committee, referred to "the question of the detention of people" and noted that McRaven had "made reference to a couple, I think, that are on a ship."

McRaven replied affirmatively, saying, "It depends on the individual case, and I'd be more than happy to discuss the cases that we've dealt with."[22]

Another press report on July 6, 2011, stated:

In a telephone briefing with reporters, senior administration officials said Mr. Warsame and another person were captured by American forces somewhere "in the Gulf region" on April 19. Another official separately said the two were picked up on a fishing trawler in international waters between Yemen and Somalia. That other person was released.

Mr. Warsame was taken to a naval vessel, where he was questioned for the next two months by military interrogators, the officials said. They said his detention was justified by the laws

---

[22] Karen DeYoung, Greg Miller, and Greg Jaffe, "Terror Suspect Detained On Ship," *Washington Post*, July 6, 2011: 6.

of war, but declined to say whether their theory was that the Shabab are covered by Congress's authorization to use military force against the perpetrators of the Sept. 11, 2001, attacks; whether the detention was justified by his interactions with Al Qaeda's Yemen branch; or something else.

The officials also said interrogators used only techniques in the Army Field Manual, which complies with the Geneva Conventions. But they did not deliver a Miranda warning because they were seeking to gather intelligence, not court evidence. One official called those sessions "very, very productive," but declined to say whether his information contributed to a drone attack in Somalia last month.

After about two months, Mr. Warsame was given a break for several days. Then a separate group of law enforcement interrogators came in. They delivered a Miranda warning, but he waived his rights to remain silent and have a lawyer present and continued to cooperate, the officials said, meaning that his subsequent statements would likely be admissible in court.

Throughout that period, administration officials were engaged in deliberations about what to do with Mr. Warsame's case. Eventually, they "unanimously" decided to prosecute him in civilian court. If he is convicted of all the charges against him, he would face life in prison.

Last week, Vice Adm. William H. McRaven, who was until recently in charge of the military's Joint Special Operations Command, told a Senate hearing that detainees are sometimes kept on Navy ships until the Justice Department can build a case against them, or they are transferred to other countries for detention.

Another senior administration official said Tuesday that such detentions are extremely rare, and that no other detainees are now being held on a Navy ship.[23]

A July 7, 2011, press report stated:

In interrogating a Somali man for months aboard a Navy ship before taking him to New York this week for a civilian trial on terrorism charges, the Obama administration is trying out a new approach for dealing with foreign terrorism suspects.

The administration, which was seeking to avoid sending a new prisoner to Guantánamo Bay, Cuba, drew praise and criticism on Wednesday [July 6] for its decisions involving the Somali suspect, Ahmed Abdulkadir Warsame, accused of aiding Al Qaeda's branch in Yemen and the Shabab, the Somali militant group.[24]

A July 6, 2011, entry in a blog that reports on naval-related events stated that the U.S. Navy ship to which Warsame was taken was the amphibious assault ship *Boxer* (LHD-4).[25]

An October 24, 2012, press report stated:

---

[23] Charlie Savage and Eric Schmitt, "U.S. To Prosecute A Somali Suspect In Civilian Court," *New York Times*, July 6, 2011: 1.

[24] Charlie Savage, "U.S. Tests New Approach To Terrorism Cases On Somali Suspect," *New York Times*, July 7, 2011: 10. See also Dave Boyer, "Interrogation At Sea Skirts Obama Pledge," *Washington Times*, July 7, 2011: 1.

[25] See "The STRATCOM [Strategic Communications] Opportunity of Ahmed Abdulkadir Warsame*," Information Dissemination (www.informationdissemination.net)*, July 6, 2011, accessed online July 6, 2011, at http://www.informationdissemination net/2011/07/stratcom-opportunity-of-ahmed.html.

Over the past two years, the Obama administration has been secretly developing a new blueprint for pursuing terrorists, a next-generation targeting list called the "disposition matrix."

The matrix contains the names of terrorism suspects arrayed against an accounting of the resources being marshaled to track them down, including sealed indictments and clandestine operations. U.S. officials said the database is designed to go beyond existing kill lists, mapping plans for the "disposition" of suspects beyond the reach of American drones.

Although the matrix is a work in progress, the effort to create it reflects a reality setting in among the nation's counterterrorism ranks: The United States' conventional wars are winding down, but the government expects to continue adding names to kill or capture lists for years....

The database is meant to map out contingencies, creating an operational menu that spells out each agency's role in case a suspect surfaces in an unexpected spot. "If he's in Saudi Arabia, pick up with the Saudis," the former official said. "If traveling overseas to al-Shabaab [in Somalia] we can pick him up by ship. If in Yemen, kill or have the Yemenis pick him up."

Officials declined to disclose the identities of suspects on the matrix. They pointed, however, to the capture last year of alleged al-Qaeda operative Ahmed Abdulkadir Warsame off the coast of Yemen. Warsame was held for two months aboard a U.S. ship before being transferred to the custody of the Justice Department and charged in federal court in New York.

"Warsame was a classic case of 'What are we going to do with him?'" the former counterterrorism official said. In such cases, the matrix lays out plans, including which U.S. naval vessels are in the vicinity and which charges the Justice Department should prepare.[26]

An October 6, 2013, press report stated:

An accused operative for Al Qaeda seized by United States commandos in Libya over the weekend is being interrogated while in military custody on a Navy ship in the Mediterranean Sea, officials said on Sunday [October 6]. He is expected eventually to be sent to New York for criminal prosecution.

The fugitive, known as Abu Anas al-Libi, is seen as a potential intelligence gold mine, possessing perhaps two decades of information about Al Qaeda, from its early days under Osama bin Laden in Sudan to its more scattered elements today.

The decision to hold Abu Anas and question him for intelligence purposes without a lawyer present follows a pattern used successfully by the Obama administration with other terrorist suspects, most prominently in the case of Ahmed Abdulkadir Warsame, a former military commander with the Somali terrorist group Shabab....

"Warsame is the model for this guy," one American security official said....

Abu Anas is being held aboard the U.S.S. San Antonio, a vessel brought in specifically for this mission, officials said.[27]

---

[26] Greg Miller, "The Permanent War, U.S. Set To Keep Kill Likes For Years," *Washington Post*, October 24, 2012: 1. Bracketed material as in original.

[27] Benjamin Weiser and Eric Schmitt, "U.S. Said to Hold Qaeda Suspect on Navy Ship," *New York Times*, October 6, (continued...)

# Navy Initiatives to Improve Its IW and CT Capabilities

The Navy in recent years has implemented a number of organizational and program initiatives intended to improve its IW and CT capabilities and activities, including those discussed below.

## Navy Irregular Warfare Office

The Navy in July 2008 established the Navy Irregular Warfare Office, which is intended, in the Navy's words, to "institutionalize current ad hoc efforts in IW missions of counterterrorism and counterinsurgency and the supporting missions of information operations, intelligence operations, foreign internal defense and unconventional warfare as they apply to [CT] and [counterinsurgency]." The office works closely with U.S. Special Operations Command, and reports to the Deputy Chief of Naval Operations for information, plans, and strategy.[28]

## 2010 Navy Vision Statement for Countering Irregular Challenges

The Navy in January 2010 published a vision statement for countering irregular challenges, which states in part:

> The U.S. Navy will meet irregular challenges through a flexible, agile, and broad array of multi-mission capabilities. We will emphasize Cooperative Security as part of a comprehensive government approach to mitigate the causes of insecurity and instability. We will operate in and from the maritime domain with joint and international partners to enhance regional security and stability, and to dissuade, deter, and when necessary, defeat irregular forces.[29]

The full text of the vision statement is reproduced in **Appendix C**.

## Navy Community of Interest for Countering Irregular Challenges

The Navy in December 2010 established "a community of interest to develop and advance ideas, collaboration and advocacy related to confronting irregular challenges (CIC)." The community, which includes a number of Navy organizations, is to be the Navy's "standing authority to facilitate: implementation of the *U.S. Navy Vision for Confronting Irregular Challenges (Vision)*; promotion of increased understanding of confronting irregular challenges; and synchronization of CIC-related initiatives within the navy and with its external partners."[30]

---

(...continued)

2013. See also Mark Hosenball and Phil Stewart, "Elite U.S. Team Questions Seized al Qaeda Leader on Navy Ship," *Reuters.com*, October 7, 3013; and "The USS Guantanamo," *Wall Street Journal*, June 22, 2014.

[28] Zachary M. Peterson, "New Navy Irregular Warfare Office Works to Address ISR Shortfall," *Inside the Navy*, September 1, 2008.

[29] Department of the Navy, Chief of Naval Operations, *The U.S. Navy's Vision for Confronting Irregular Challenges*, January 2010, p. 3.

[30] Source: Memorandum dated December 22, 2010, from S. M. Harris, Director, Navy Irregular Warfare Office, on the subject, "Confronting Irregular Challenges Community of Interest (COI) Charter." A copy of the memorandum was posted at InsideDefense.com (subscription required). For an article discussing the Navy's establishment of this community of interest, see Christopher J. Castelli, "Navy Taps Other Services, Elite Forces For Irregular Warfare Advice," *Inside the Navy*, January 17, 2011.

---

## Navy Expeditionary Combat Command (NECC)

The Navy Expeditionary Combat Command (NECC), headquartered at Naval Amphibious Base, Little Creek, VA, was established informally in October 2005 and formally on January 13, 2006. NECC consolidated and facilitated the expansion of a number of Navy organizations that have a role in IW operations. Navy functions supported by NECC include the following:

- riverine warfare;
- maritime civil affairs;
- expeditionary training;
- explosive ordnance disposal (EOD);
- expeditionary intelligence;
- naval construction (i.e., the naval construction brigades, aka CBs or "Seabee");
- maritime expeditionary security;
- expeditionary diving;
- combat camera;
- expeditionary logistics;
- guard battalion; and
- expeditionary combat readiness.

DON states that:

> Navy Expeditionary Combat Command (NECC) is a global force provider of expeditionary combat service support and force protection capabilities to joint warfighting commanders. It is responsible for centrally managing the current and future readiness, resources, manning, training and equipping of a scalable, self-sustaining, integrated expeditionary force of active and reserve sailors. Expeditionary sailors are deployed from around the globe, supporting contingency operations and Combatant Commanders' Theater Security Cooperation Plans, providing a forward presence of waterborne and ashore anti-terrorism force protection; theater security cooperation and engagement; and humanitarian assistance and disaster relief.[31]

DON also states that

> The Reserve Component expeditionary forces are integrated with the Active Component forces to provide a continuum of capabilities unique to the maritime environment within NECC. Blending the AC and RC brings strength to the force and is an important part of the Navy's ability to carry out the Naval Maritime Strategy from blue water into green and brown water and in direct support of the Joint Force. The Navy Reserve trains and equips over half of the Sailors supporting NECC missions, including naval construction and explosive ordnance disposal in the CENTCOM region, as well as maritime expeditionary security, expeditionary logistics (cargo handling battalions), maritime civil affairs, expeditionary intelligence, and other mission capabilities seamlessly integrated with

---

[31] Department of the Navy, *Highlights of the Department of the Navy FY 2015 Budget*, 2014, pp. 3-12 and 3-13.

operational forces around the world. In addition, Coastal Riverine Group 2 has taken on a new armed escort mission for High Value Units (HVU) which has traditionally been provided by the U.S. Coast Guard. The escort enhances force protection for HVUs while transiting into and out of CONUS ports during restricted maneuvering.[32]

On October 1, 2012, the Navy established NECC Pacific (NECC PAC) "to provide administrative control for Navy expeditionary forces assigned to the Pacific theater." The new organization, the Navy says, "formalizes a direct administrative relationship between NECC and Commander, U.S. Pacific Fleet—a linkage that hasn't existed since NECC's establishment in 2006."[33]

## Global Maritime Partnership

The Global Maritime Partnership is a U.S. Navy initiative to achieve an enhanced degree of cooperation between the U.S. Navy and foreign navies, coast guards, and maritime police forces, for the purpose of ensuring global maritime security against common threats. DON states, "Through partnerships with a growing number of nations, including those in Africa and Latin America, we will strive for a common vision of freedom, stability, and prosperity."[34]

## Partnership Stations

The Southern Partnership Station (SPS) and the Africa Partnership Station (APS) are Navy ships, such as amphibious ships or high-speed sealift ships, that have deployed to the Caribbean and to waters off Africa, respectively, to support U.S. Navy engagement with countries in those regions, particularly for purposes of building security partnerships with those countries, and for increasing the capabilities of those countries for performing maritime-security operations. The SPS and APS can be viewed as specific measures for promoting the above-discussed global maritime partnership. A July 2010 Government Accountability Office (GAO) report discussed the APS.[35]

## Coastal Riverine Force

The Navy in May 2006 reestablished its riverine force by standing up Riverine Group 1 at Naval Amphibious Base, Little Creek, VA (now part of Joint Expeditionary Base Little Creek-Fort Story, or JEBLC-FS). Riverine Group 1 included three active-duty riverine squadrons of 12 boats each that were established in 2006-2007. Operations of the squadrons from 2006 to 2011 included multiple deployments to Iraq for the purpose, among other things, of relieving Marines who until 2006 had been conducting maritime security operations in Iraqi ports and waterways.

On June 1, 2012, the Navy merged the riverine force and the Maritime Expeditionary Security Force (MESF) to create Coastal Riverine Force (CORIVFOR). The Navy states that CORIVFOR

---

[32] Department of the Navy, *Highlights of the Department of the Navy FY 2015 Budget*, 2014, p. 3-20.

[33] Navy Expeditionary Combat Command Public Affairs, "#Warfighting: Navy Expeditionary Combat Command Pacific Established," *Navy News Service*, October 3, 2012, accessed October 18, 2012, at http://www navy mil/submit/display.asp?story_id=69947.

[34] Department of the Navy, *Highlights of the Department of the Navy FY 2015 Budget*, 2014, p. 7-1. For more on the Navy's contribution to multinational antipiracy operations near the Horn of Africa, see CRS Report R40528, *Piracy off the Horn of Africa*, by Lauren Ploch Blanchard et al.

[35] Government Accountability Office, *Defense Management[:]Improved Planning, Training, and Interagency Collaboration Could Strengthen DOD's Efforts in Africa*, GAO-10-794, July 2010, 63 pp.

"performs core maritime expeditionary security missions in the green and brown waters, bridging the gap between traditional Navy blue water operations and land-based forces, providing port and harbor security for vital waterways and protection of high value assets and maritime infrastructure."[36] The Navy stated that CORIVFOR was scheduled to reach initial operating capability (IOC) in October 2012 and full operational capability (FOC) in October 2014, and that "all current and scheduled routine deployments will continue as normal."[37]

CORIVFOR consists of about 2,500 active-duty sailors and 2,000 reserve sailors, and includes Coastal Riverine Groups (CORIVGRUs) 1 and 2. CORIVGRU 1 is homeported at Imperial Beach, CA, with squadrons located at the Naval Amphibious Base in San Diego. CORIVGRU 2 is homeported at Portsmouth, VA, with active-duty squadrons located at Norfolk Naval Shipyard at Portsmouth, VA, JEBLC-FS, and a forward-deployed detachment in Bahrain, and with reserve squadrons located at Newport, RI, and Jacksonville, FL.[38] On August 1, 2012, the Navy established Coastal Riverine Squadron (CORIVRON) 4, merging Riverine Squadron (RIVRON) 1 and Maritime Expeditionary Security Squadron (MSRON) 4. CORIVRON 1 is the first squadron to merge since the establishment of CORIVFOR.[39]

A November 1, 2012, press report stated:

> In Iraq, Riverine forces became a quick reaction force—capable of search-and-seizure, insertion or extraction—on swift, agile boats with heavy-caliber weaponry. Between March 2007 and October 2011, the Riverines carried out more than 2,000 missions, trained Iraqi River Police, screened detainees and discovered weapons caches while flying 667 unmanned aerial vehicle hours.
>
> Army and Navy river units were dismantled after the Vietnam War ended in 1975 and the Riverines's future was in limbo when the Iraq war wound down last year. The Navy, however, has decided it has an enduring need for these quick and lethal small boat fighters....
>
> The Navy has decided to merge the more offensive Riverine Group 1 and the more defensive Maritime Expeditionary Security Force to form the Coastal Riverine Force. The hybrid command is designed to operate in rivers, coastal waterways and possibly even in open ocean, bridging the gap between land-based forces and the Navy ships that operate off the coast.
>
> The 5,000-strong force should be up and running initially this month, a Navy statement said, although it is not expected to be fully merged and operational for two years.

---

[36] Kay Savarese, "NECC Establishes Coast Riverine Force," *Navy News Service*, June 1, 2012, accessed June 27, 2012, at http://www.navy.mil/submit/display.asp?story_id=67545. See also Corinne Reilly, "New Navy Command To Incorporate Riverines," *Norfolk Virginian-Pilot*, May 16, 2012; Megan Eckstein, "Coastal Riverine Force Expanding Its Reach Following June 1 Merger," *Inside the Navy*, June 11, 2012; and Christopher P. Cavas, "U.S. Navy Reorganizes Post-War Riverine Forces," *Defense News*, May 7, 2012: 4.

[37] Naval Expeditionary Combat Command Public Affairs, "NECC Announces Formation of Coastal Riverine Force," Navy News Service, May 14, 2012, accessed May 15, 2012, at http://www.navy mil/submit/display.asp?story_id= 67167.

[38] Kay Savarese, "NECC Establishes Coast Riverine Force," *Navy News Service*, June 1, 2012, accessed June 27, 2012, at http://www.navy.mil/submit/display.asp?story_id=67545.

[39] Steven C. Hoskins, "Coastal Riverine Force Establishes Squadron," *Navy News Service*, August 2, 2012, accessed October 18, 2012, at http://www.navy.mil/submit/display.asp?story_id=68790.

It will be broken up into two groups. Coastal Riverine Group 1 will be based at Imperial Beach, Calif., with a squadron at the Naval Amphibious Base in San Diego. Coastal Riverine Group 2 will have its headquarters in Portsmouth, Va., with additional squadrons in Bahrain, Rhode Island and Florida.

Each squadron will feature a headquarters element and four distinct companies, three of which will handle security operations, to include protecting ships and shore facilities, carrying out search-and seizure-operations and providing security for aircraft.

The fourth, Delta company, will specialize in traditional Riverine duties, such as insertions and extractions, boardings on rivers and other inland waters, intelligence collection and more offensive combat operations, said Capt. James Hamblet, Coastal Riverine Group 2's commander.

The new force will focus primarily in the Navy's 5th Fleet area of operations, which includes the Persian Gulf and waterways, Navy Expeditionary Combat Command skipper Rear Adm. Michael Tillotson said at the establishment ceremony for Coastal Riverine Group 2 in June. But, he expects that focus to shift to the Pacific over time.

"We will work with partners along the areas known as Oceana, which includes Indonesia, Papua New Guinea and Malaysia; we'll work in the areas and help build relationships with those countries in order to provide security in those areas," Tillotson said. "The challenges are out there."

The force features a mix of maritime expeditionary security and Riverine gear and apparatus, with plans to obtain more advanced craft in the future. The Coastal Riverines now operate 113 boats, ranging from rubber combat raiding crafts to 53-foot command boats that can carry up to 26 personnel. The force has 2,657 active and 2,507 Reserve personnel, Navy Expeditionary Combat Command spokeswoman Barbara Wilcox wrote to Stars and Stripes.

The force's future is the MK-VI patrol boat, which will allow Coastal Riverine sailors the ability to operate farther off the coast and will improve boarding capabilities as it is brought into service, Hamblet said. The 78-foot boat is capable of speeds in excess 30 knots with twin diesel engines and water jets. It has a range of 600 nautical miles.[40]

A January 18, 2013, Navy news report stated:

Sailors, former Riverines, and family members attended a disestablishment ceremony for Naval Expeditionary Combat Command's Riverine Squadron (RIVRON) 3 at Naval Weapons Station Yorktown, Jan. 17.

The disestablishment marks the merger of offensive Riverine forces with defensive Maritime Expeditionary Security Forces to form the Coastal Riverine Force (CORIVFOR), formally established June 1[, 2012]....

CORIVFOR's primary mission is to conduct maritime security operations across all phases of military operations by defending high value assets, critical maritime infrastructure, ports and harbors, both inland and on coastal waterways, and when commanded, conduct offensive combat operations.

---

[40] Matthew M. Burke, "Reviving the Roverines," *Stars and Stripes*, November 1, 2012: 1.

The budget-initiated merger moved portions of the force to San Diego as part of the National Defense Strategy's rebalance to the Pacific, which will bring Riverine capability to the West coast for the first time since 1974, according to Capt. Eric B. Moss, commander of Coastal Riverine Group 1, formerly Maritime Expeditionary Security Group 1.

"The Riverine forces will do what they've always done, which is continuing to hone their skills and work in brown water and green water areas," said Moss. "There is no abatement of requirements. We continue to get missions and are sourced to meet those requirements. We're doing the same with less."

The merge cuts the former seven active Maritime Expeditionary Security Force (MESF) squadrons and three active RIVRONs down to three active Coastal Riverine squadrons and four reserve squadrons.

"This is a reduction in capacity, but not in capability," said Moss. "I would say this is a very affordable force. We are light, expeditionary, and bring a lot capability in small packages. We are familiar with disaggregated operations, so immediately we give the combatant commander a tailor-able and scalable force."...

Commissioned July 6, 2007, RIVRON 3 served two deployments in Iraq, fulfilling a total of 502 combat missions, 268 water security operations and countless U.S./Iraq tactical convoy operations.[41]

## Other Organizational Initiatives

Other Navy initiatives in recent years for supporting IW and CT operations include establishing a reserve civil affairs battalion, a Navy Foreign Area Officer (FAO) community consisting of officers with specialized knowledge of foreign countries and regions, a maritime interception operation (MIO) intelligence exploitation pilot program, and an intelligence data-mining capability at the National Maritime Intelligence Center (NMIC).

# FY2015 Funding Request

DOD's proposed FY2015 defense budget requests, among other things, $25.459 million for underwater systems for the Special Operations Command (SOCOM) in the Procurement, Defense-Wide appropriation account, compared to $15.439 million for this line item in FY2014 and $5.936 million in FY2013. DOD states that

The Underwater Systems line item procures dry and wet combat submersibles, technology insertions for the SEAL Delivery Vehicle (SDV) fleet, and modifications and field changes to the Dry Deck Shelter (DDS). Acquisition procurement programs of record that will continue are the Shallow Water Combat Submersible (SWCS) program and modifications to the current Dry Deck Shelter (DDS). The SDV procurement funding for obsolescence upgrades ended in FY 2013. SWCS Block 1 is the next generation free-flooding combat submersible that transports Special Operations Forces (SOF) personnel and their combat equipment in hostile waters for a variety of missions. SOF units require specialized underwater systems that improve their warfighting capability and survivability in harsh operating environments. The Dry Combat Submersibles (DCS) will provide the capability to

---

[41] Shannon M. Smith, "RIVRON 3 Disestablishes at Naval Weapon Station Yorktown," *Navy News Service*, January 18, 2013.

insert and extract SOF and/or payloads into denied areas from strategic distances. The program is structured to minimize technical, cost, and schedule risks by leveraging commercial technologies, procedures and classing methods to achieve an affordable DCS. Other examples of underwater systems and maritime equipment include, but may not be limited to underwater navigation, diving equipment, and underwater propulsion systems.

Systems and equipment are used in the conduct of infiltration/extraction, reconnaissance, beach obstacle clearance, and other missions. The capabilities of submersible systems and unique equipment provides small, highly trained forces the ability to successfully engage the enemy and conduct operations associated with SOF maritime missions....

**Justification:**

1. DDS. The DDS is a certified diving system that attaches to modified host submarines. Program provides certification, field changes, and minor modifications for the DDS. This program was reduced in FY 2013 by $0.295 million due to sequestration.

FY 2015 PROGRAM JUSTIFICATION: Funds minor modification efforts and field changes to the current class of six DDS's that are in service with the US Navy. Funding continues engineering design, fabrication, assembly, acceptance, and testing for field change kits. Includes changes for relocation of equipment inside the DDS hangar to accommodate SWCS Block 1, also includes field changes for items such as camera replacements, gauge replacements, mechanical quieting, lighting upgrades, and other general field changes to support deficiency resolution.

2. SDV. The SDV is a small battery-powered, free-flooding combat submersible that transports SOF personnel and their combat equipment in hostile waters. This program corrects sustainability and maintainability issues within subsystems in response to obsolescence of imbedded commercial-off-the-shelf electronics hardware and software. FY 2013 is last year of procurement funding for SDV obsolescence upgrades. This program was reduced in FY 2013 by $0.240 million due to sequestration.

3. SWCS (Block 1). The SWCS (Block 1) is the replacement for the SEAL Delivery Vehicle. SWCS (Block 1) is the next generation free-flooding combat submersible that transports SOF personnel and their combat equipment in hostile waters for a variety of missions. FY 2014 is the first year of procurement funds for the replacement system and provides government furnished equipment (GFE) such as Satellite Communications antennas, batteries, docking sonar and radios.

FY 2015 PROGRAM JUSTIFICATION: Purchases up to two SWCS (Block 1) vehicles, batteries, trailers, and GFE, initial spares.

4. Dry Combatant Submersible (DCS). The DCS craft provides SOF with a diver lock-in and lock-out capability; that transports personnel and their combat equipment in hostile waters for a variety of missions.[42]

DON states:

The MQ-8 VTUAV [Vertical Take Off and Landing Tactical Unmanned Aerial Vehicle] conducts missions including over-the-horizon tactical reconnaissance, classification,

---

[42] *Department of Defense Fiscal Year (FY) 2015 Budget Estimates, United States Special Operations Command, Defense Wide Justification Book, Volume 1 of 2, Procurement, Defense-Wide*, March 2014, pp. 113-114.

targeting, laser designation, and battle management. The MQ-8 launches and recovers vertically and can operate from air capable ships (DDG, CG, FFG, LCS) [destroyers, cruisers, frigates, Littoral Combat Ships], as well as confined area land bases. The Department has discontinued planned support for Special Operations Force ISR [intelligence, surveillance, and reconnaissance] requirements. Future MQ-8C operations will focus on integration with LCS operations.[43]

# Potential Oversight Issues for Congress

## Degree of Emphasis on IW and CT in Future Navy Budgets

One potential oversight issue for Congress is how much emphasis to place on IW and CT activities in future Navy budgets, particularly in the context of potential constraints on future DOD budgets and the U.S. strategic rebalancing toward the Asia-Pacific region. Supporters of placing continued or increased emphasis on IW and CT activities in future Navy budgets could cite continued threats to U.S. interests from terrorist organizations and Navy-unique IW and CT capabilities that need to be supported as part of an effective overall U.S. IW or CT effort. Supporters of placing a reduced emphasis on emphasis on IW and CT activities in future Navy budgets could cite the end of U.S. military operations in Iraq, the winding down of U.S. military operations in Afghanistan, and the need to fund programs for conventional Navy warfighting capabilities for countering improved Chinese military capabilities. Potential oversight questions for Congress include the following:

- To what degree can or should Navy IW and CT activities be used to reduce the burden on other services for conducting such activities?

- Is the Navy striking an appropriate balance between IW and CT activities and other Navy concerns, such as preparing for a potential future challenge from improved Chinese maritime military forces?[44]

## Additional Oversight Questions

In addition to the issues discussed above, the Navy's IW and CT activities pose some additional potential oversight issues for Congress, including the following:

- How many Navy personnel globally are involved in IW and CT activities, and where are they located? How much funding is the Navy expending each year on such activities?

- Is the Navy adequately managing its individual augmentee (IA) program?[45]

- Is the Navy devoting sufficient attention and resources to riverine warfare?[46]

---

[43] Department of the Navy, *Highlights of the Department of the Navy FY 2015 Budget*, 2014, p. 4-11.

[44] For additional discussion of this issue, see CRS Report RL33153, *China Naval Modernization: Implications for U.S. Navy Capabilities—Background and Issues for Congress*, by Ronald O'Rourke.

[45] For a discussion of the Navy's management of the IA program, see Andrew Scutro, "Fleet Forces Takes Charge of IA Program," *NavyTimes.com*, July 7, 2008.

[46] For an article that discusses this question from a critical perspective, see Daniel A. Hancock, "The Navy's Not (continued...)

- Is the Navy adequately coordinating its IW and CT activities and initiatives with other organizations, such as the Special Operations Command (SOCOM) and the Coast Guard?

- Are the Navy's recent IW and CT organizational changes appropriate? What other Navy organizational changes might be needed?

# Legislative Activity for FY2015

## FY2015 National Defense Authorization Act (H.R. 4435/S. 2410)

### House

The House Armed Services Committee, in its report (H.Rept. 113-446 of May 13, 2014) on H.R. 4435, recommends approving DOD's request for $25.459 million for underwater systems for the Special Operations Command (SOCOM) in the Procurement, Defense-Wide appropriation account. (Page 416, line 063.)

**Section 123** of H.R. 4435 as reported states:

> SEC. 123. ADDITIONAL OVERSIGHT REQUIREMENTS FOR THE UNDERSEA MOBILITY ACQUISITION PROGRAM OF THE UNITED STATES SPECIAL OPERATIONS COMMAND.
>
> (a) Limitation on Milestone B Decision- The Commander of the United States Special Operations Command may not make any Milestone B acquisition decisions with respect to a covered element unless—
>
> (1) the Commander has submitted to the congressional defense committees the transition plan under subsection (b)(2);
>
> (2) the Under Secretary of Defense for Acquisition, Technology, and Logistics has submitted to such committees the certification under subsection (c)(1); and
>
> (3) the Secretary of the Navy has completed the review under subsection (d)(1).
>
> (b) Transition Plan-
>
> (1) IN GENERAL- The Commander shall develop a transition plan for undersea mobility capabilities that includes the following:
>
> (A) A description of the current capabilities provided by covered elements as of the date of the plan.
>
> (B) An identification and description of the requirements of the Commander for future undersea mobility platforms.

---

(...continued)

Serious About Riverine Warfare," *U.S. Naval Institute Proceedings*, January 2008: 14-19.

(C) An identification of resources necessary to fulfill the requirements identified in subparagraph (B).

(D) A description of the technology readiness levels of any covered element currently under development as of the date of the plan.

(E) An identification of any potential gaps or projected shortfall in capability, along with steps to mitigate any such gap or shortfall.

(F) Any other matters the Commander determines appropriate.

(2) SUBMISSION- The Commander shall submit to the congressional defense committees the transition plan under paragraph (1).

(c) Certification-

(1) IN GENERAL- Except as provided by paragraph (2), the Under Secretary of Defense for Acquisition, Technology, and Logistics shall certify an acquisition strategy for covered elements developed by the Commander if such strategy—

(A) is based on reasonable cost and schedule estimates to execute the product development and production plan;

(B) the technology in the program has been demonstrated in a relevant environment; and

(C) the program complies with all relevant policies, regulations, and directives of the Secretary of Defense.

(2) WAIVER- The Secretary of Defense may waive the certification requirement in paragraph (1) if the Secretary—

(A) determines that such certification is not in the interests of the United States; and

(B) notifies the congressional defense committees of such determination, including justifications for making the waiver.

(d) Review- The Secretary of the Navy shall—

(1) review the transition plan under subsection (b)(1) and the acquisition strategy described in subsection (c)(1); and

(2) ensure that the development of requirements for the Navy and the acquisition plans of the Navy take into account such transition plan and acquisition strategy.

(e) Definitions- In this section:

(1) The term `covered element' means any of the following elements of the undersea mobility acquisition program of the United States Special Operations Command:

(A) The dry combat submersible-light program.

(B) The dry combat submersible-medium program.

(C) The next-generation submarine shelter program.

(D) Any new dry combat submersible developed under the undersea mobility acquisition program of the United States Special Operations Command after the date of the enactment of this Act.

(2) The term 'Milestone B approval' has the meaning given that term in section 2366(e) of title 10, United States Code.

(f) Conforming Repeal- Section 144 of the National Defense Authorization Act for Fiscal Year 2012 (P.L. 112-81; 125 Stat. 1325) is repealed.[47]

H.Rept. 113-446 states:

> United States Special Operations Command Proposed Sponsorship of U.S. Naval Ship Sumner
>
> The committee is aware that the United States Special Operations Command (USSOCOM) recently requested transfer of sponsorship of the United States Naval Ship (USNS) Sumner (T–AGS 61) from the Military Sealift Command to USSOCOM to support near-term

---

[47] Section 144 of H.R. 1540/P.L. 112-81 of December 31, 2011, the FY2012 National Defense Authorization Act, states:

> SEC. 144. ADDITIONAL OVERSIGHT REQUIREMENTS FOR THE UNDERSEA MOBILITY ACQUISITION PROGRAM OF THE UNITED STATES SPECIAL OPERATIONS COMMAND.
>
> (a) Limitation on Milestone B Decision- The Commander of the United States Special Operations Command may not make any milestone B acquisition decisions with respect to a covered element until a 30-day period has elapsed after the date on which the Under Secretary of Defense for Acquisition, Technology, and Logistics—
>
> (1) conducts the assessment and determination under subsection (b) for the covered element; and
>
> (2) submits to the congressional defense committees a report including—
>
> (A) the determination of the Under Secretary with respect to the appropriate acquisition category for the covered element; and
>
> (B) the validated requirements, independent cost estimate, test and evaluation master plan, and technology readiness assessment described in paragraphs (1) through (4) of subsection (b), respectively.
>
> (b) Assessment and Determination- With respect to each covered element, the Under Secretary shall conduct an assessment and determination of whether to treat the covered element as a major defense acquisition program. Such assessment shall include—
>
> (1) a requirements validation by the Joint Requirements Oversight Council;
>
> (2) an independent cost estimate prepared by the Director of Cost Assessment and Program Evaluation;
>
> (3) a test and evaluation master plan reviewed by the Director of Operational Test and Evaluation; and
>
> (4) a technology readiness assessment reviewed by the Assistant Secretary of Defense for Research and Engineering.
>
> (c) Covered Element Defined- In this section, the term 'covered element' means any of the following elements of the undersea mobility acquisition program of the United States Special Operations Command:
>
> (1) The dry combat submersible-light program.
>
> (2) The dry combat submersible-medium program.
>
> (3) The next-generation submarine shelter program.
>
> (4) Any new dry combat submersible developed under the undersea mobility acquisition program of the United States Special Operations Command after the date of the enactment of this Act.

---

maritime requirements for United States Southern Command. The committee is also aware that USSOCOM has initiated a new-start procurement using current fiscal year 2014 funds to begin modifications to USNS Sumner estimated at $8.9 million. The budget request for fiscal year 2015 included $20.3 million in Operation and Maintenance, Defense-wide, to further modify and operate USNS Sumner within the United States Southern Command area of operations.

The committee is concerned that the proposed transfer of sponsorship of USNS Sumner to USSOCOM and proposed command and control relationships are without precedent, and that projected costs for the current fiscal year and across the Future Years Defense Program will far exceed current estimates. Further, the committee has concerns that the requirement is being funded only by USSOCOM Major Force Program–11 (MFP–11) funds which are limited by section 167 of title 10, United States Code, to provide only the incremental funding and acquisition of special operations-peculiar material, supplies, and services. Since the committee understands that this platform will be used to also support the geographic combatant commander theater campaign plans such as counter-narcotics, humanitarian assistance, and security force assistance, the committee believes that MFP–11 funding is an inappropriate source for these costly modifications and operations, and that MFP–11 is being used to supplant activities that should be provided for by the services and the geographic combatant commander.

Therefore, the committee directs the Secretary of Defense to provide a briefing to the congressional defense committees by August 1, 2014, on the proposed transfer of the USNS Sumner from Military Sealift Command to USSOCOM. The briefing at a minimum should outline:

(1) The validated requirement as defined by the geographic combatant commander;

(2) Anticipated costs across the Future Years Defense Program and funding sources;

(3) Reason for the use of USNS Sumner, to include a business case analysis discussing efficiencies and cost savings; and

(4) Any other matters the Secretary deems appropriate.

Furthermore, given these concerns, the committee denies the requested amount of $20.3 million in Operation and Maintenance, Defense-wide, to further modify and operate USNS Sumner and redirects this funding to more direct operational readiness requirements within Operation and Maintenance, Defense-wide, Flying Hours Program for USSOCOM. (Pages 129-130)

## Senate

The Senate Armed Services Committee, in its report (S.Rept. 113-176 of June 2, 2014) on S. 2410, recommends approving DOD's request for $25.459 million for underwater systems for the Special Operations Command (SOCOM) in the Procurement, Defense-Wide appropriation account. (Page 344, line 63.)

# FY2015 DOD Appropriations Act (H.R. 4870)

## House

The House Appropriations Committee, in its report (H.Rept. 113-473 of June 13, 2014) on H.R. 4870, recommends approving DOD's request for $25.459 million for underwater systems for the Special Operations Command (SOCOM) in the Procurement, Defense-Wide appropriation account. (Page 204, line 63.)

# Appendix A. November 2011 Navy Testimony on Navy IW Activities

Below is the text of the Navy's prepared statement for a November 3, 2011, hearing before the Emerging Threats and Capabilities subcommittee of the House Armed Services Committee on the IW activities of the military services. The text of the statement, by Rear Admiral Sinclair Harris, Director, Navy Irregular Warfare Office, is as follows:

Chairman Thornberry, Congressman Langevin, and distinguished members of the House Armed Services Emerging Threats and Capabilities Subcommittee, it is an honor for me to be here with you today to address the U.S. Navy's efforts to institutionalize and develop proficiency in irregular warfare mission areas. These efforts are vital to our national interests and, as part of a comprehensive approach for meeting complex global challenges, remain relevant in a time of uncertainty and constant change. To meet these challenges Admiral Greenert, Chief of Naval Operations, recently provided his Sailing Directions to our Navy emphasizing the mission to deter aggression and, if deterrence fails, to win our Nation's wars. Today, the Navy is engaged around the world conducting preventive activities that stabilize, strengthen, and secure our partners and allies providing regional deterrence against state and non-state actors, while at the same time fighting, and winning, our Nation's wars. We expect the demand for these activities to increase in the future security environment as a capacity constrained Navy seeks to maintain access and presence. Emphasis on increased training and education will enable our continued readiness to effectively meet global demand.

As demand for our Navy continues to grow, we continue to leverage our Maritime Strategy with our partners, the Marine Corps and Coast Guard. The maritime domain supports 90% of the world's trade and provides offshore options to help friends in need, and to confront and defeat aggression far from our shores as part of a defense in depth approach to secure our homeland. CNO's Sailing Directions, coupled with an enduring Maritime Strategy, underscore the Navy's focus on multi-mission platforms and highly trained Sailors that conduct activities across the operational spectrum. Key tenets of the force are readiness to fight and win today while building the ability to win tomorrow; to provide offshore options to deter, influence, and win; and to harness the teamwork, talent and imagination of our diverse force. While the Maritime Strategy spans the spectrum of warfare, the Navy's Vision for Confronting Irregular Challenges (CIC), released in January 2010, addresses mission areas of irregular warfare as well as maritime activities to prevent, limit, and interdict irregular threats and their influence on regional stability through, insurgency, crime, and violent extremism.

The CIC Vision is derived from our Maritime Strategy with the intention to implement steps towards increasing the Navy's proficiency in supporting direct and indirect approaches that dissuade and defeat irregular actors who exploit uncontrolled or ungoverned spaces in order to employ informational, economic, technological, and kinetic means against civilian populations to achieve their objectives. The CIC Vision is guiding the alignment of organizations, investments, innovation, procedures, doctrine, and training needed to mainstream CIC capabilities within the Fleet. These efforts are focused on outcomes of increased effectiveness in stabilizing and strengthening regions, enhancing regional awareness, increasing regional maritime partner capacity, and expanding coordination and interoperability with joint, interagency, and international partners. These outcomes support promoting regional security and stability and advancing the rule of law allowing good governance and promoting prosperity by helping partners better protect their people and resources. In addition to preventive activities, the Vision guides efforts to inhibit the spread of violent extremism and illicit, terrorist, and insurgent activities. To achieve these outcomes, the Navy is actively reorienting doctrine and operational approaches, rebalancing investments and developmental efforts, and refining operations and partnerships to better support a comprehensive approach to U.S. efforts. These efforts will provide a Navy capable of confronting irregular challenges through a broad array of multi-mission capabilities and a force proficient in the CIC missions of security force assistance, maritime security, stability operations, information dominance, and force application necessary to support counterinsurgency, counterterrorism, and foreign internal defense missions.

In line with its strategy for confronting irregular challenges the Navy has leveraged key force providers, such as the Navy Expeditionary Combat Command, and established Maritime Partnership Stations, and Maritime Headquarters with Maritime Operations Centers to meet the demands and missions consistent with its strategy and vision. The evolution of intelligence and strike capabilities has enabled the Navy to meet urgent Combatant Commander requirements for counterterrorism and counterinsurgency operations and highlighted further opportunities for the Navy as an important joint partner. While these operational organizations and activities deliver Navy capabilities in theater, the Navy Irregular Warfare Office, established by the CNO in July 2008, has guided the implementation and institutionalization of the CIC Vision. The Navy Irregular Warfare Office, working closely with USSOCOM, other Combatant Commanders, Services, interagency and international partners, has rapidly identified and deployed Navy capabilities to today's fight, and is institutionalizing confronting irregular challenges concepts in the Navy's planning, investment, and capability development.

The Navy Irregular Warfare Office operates under three primary imperatives consistent with the Maritime Strategy, CNO's Sailing Directions, and the Navy's Vision for Confronting Irregular Challenges. They provide integration and institutionalization in CIC mission areas and are; (1) improve the level of understanding concerning the maritime contribution to the joint force; (2) increase proficiency of the whole of Navy to confront irregular challenges; and (3) drive maritime and special operations forces to seamless integration in addressing irregular challenges. These three imperatives focus the Navy's implementation efforts and mainstream the concept that preventing wars is as important as winning them. Our Navy must be ready to transition seamlessly between operational environments, with the capability and training inherent in the Fleet.

Department of Defense Directive 3000.07 directs the services to "improve DoD proficiency for irregular warfare, which also enhances its conduct of stability operations" and directs reporting to the Chairman of the Joint Chiefs of Staff annually. Navy efforts to institutionalize and provide proficiency in confronting irregular challenges, includes proficiency in irregular warfare missions along with missions of maritime security operations and information dominance, a key enabler for CIC. Currently, the Navy leverages its access and persistent presence to both better understand and respond to irregular challenges and is actively evolving its proficiency to prevent and counter irregular threats while maintaining its ability to conduct the full spectrum of naval warfare. Its access, presence, and emphasis on maritime partnerships enable broader government efforts to address underlying conditions of instability that enhance regional security. Through its mix of multi-mission capabilities, the Navy provides political leaders with a range of offshore options for limiting regional conflict through assurance, deterrence, escalation and de-escalation, gaining and maintaining access, and rapid crisis response. In addition to its inherent ability to protect the maritime commons, its effectiveness in building maritime partner capability and capacity contributes to achieving partner security and economic objectives. Operating in and from the maritime domain with joint and international partners, the Navy is enhancing regional security while dissuading, deterring, and when necessary, defeating irregular threats.

The Navy acknowledges the complexity of the future security environment and continues to explore balanced approaches. Following are the Navy's current focus areas:

Fleet-SOF Integration: Navy's afloat basing support to special operations forces has extended their reach into denied or semi-permissive areas enabling highly successful counterterrorism missions. Navy provides inherent combat capabilities, multi-mission ships and submarines collecting mission critical information, approval for 1052 support billets for Naval Special Warfare, two dedicated HCS squadrons, and shipboard controlled UAV orbits supporting counterterrorism operations. The Navy is aligned to improve this integration through pre-deployment training, mission rehearsals, improvements to fleet bandwidth allocation, shipboard C4I enhancements, and C2 relationships needed to prosecute time sensitive targets.

Maritime Partnerships: Establishing enduring maritime partnerships is a long-term strategy for securing the maritime commons. Legal, jurisdictional, and diplomatic considerations often complicate efforts to secure the maritime commons, especially from exploitation by highly adaptive irregular actors. In recognition of these considerations, the Navy is emphasizing partnership engagements with U.S. and international maritime forces to strengthen regional security.

Information Sharing Initiatives: In an information dominated environment, initiatives that link joint warfighters, the technology community, and academia are crucial to rapidly fielding solutions to emerging irregular challenges. These initiatives are the basis for longer-term efforts to adapt and improve proficiency of Navy platforms to address irregular challenges.

Doctrine: Development of Tri-Service (Navy, Marine Corps, and Coast Guard) Maritime Stability Operations doctrine that will enable a more effective response to instability in the littorals.

Organization: Navy Expeditionary Combat Command, which continues to provide in-demand capabilities such as Maritime Civil Affairs Teams, Riverine Forces, Maritime Security Forces, Explosive Ordnance Disposal Teams, and Expeditionary Intelligence Teams.

Today, the Navy continues to meet planned global operational commitments and respond to crises as they emerge. Overseas Contingency Operations continue with more than 12,000 active and reserve Sailors serving around the globe and another 15,000 at sea in Central Command. Navy's Carrier Strike Groups provide 30 percent of the close air support for troops on the ground in Afghanistan and our Navy and Marine Corps pilots fly almost 60% of electronic attack missions. Yet, as our national interests extend beyond Iraq and Afghanistan, so do the operations of our Navy. Over the last year, more than 50 percent of our Navy has been underway daily; globally present, and persistently engaged. Last year, our Navy conducted counter-piracy operations in the Indian Ocean and North Arabian Sea with a coalition of several nations, trained local forces in maritime security as part of our Global Maritime Partnership initiatives in Europe, South America, Africa and the Pacific and forces in the Sixth Fleet supported NATO in complex operations in Libya. Navy responded with humanitarian assistance and disaster relief to the earthquake in Haiti, the flooding in Pakistan, and the earthquake and tsunami in Japan; and, conducted the world's largest maritime exercise, Rim of the Pacific (RIMPAC), which brought together 14 nations and more than 20,000 military personnel, to improve coordination and trust in multi-national operations in the Pacific. Our Sailors continue to deploy forward throughout the world, projecting US influence, responding to contingencies, and building international relationships that enable the safe, secure, and free flow of commerce that underpins our economic prosperity and advances the mission areas that address irregular challenges.

The future vision of the Navy in meeting the uncertain challenges around the globe remains a force forward, present, and persistent in areas critical to the national interests of the United States. CNO, in previous testimony,[48] stated: *Our Navy continues to conduct a high tempo of global operations, which we expect to continue even as forces draw down in Afghanistan. Global trends in economics, demographics, resources, and climate change portend an increased demand for maritime presence, power, and influence. America's prosperity depends on the seas... and as disruption and disorder persist in our security environment, maritime activity will evolve and expand. Seapower allows our nation to maintain U.S. presence and influence globally and, when necessary, project power without a costly, sizeable, or permanent footprint ashore. We will continue to maintain a forward-deployed presence around the world to prevent conflict, increase interoperability with our allies, enhance the maritime security and capacity of our traditional and emerging partners, confront irregular challenges, and respond to crises.* To continue as a global force in the preventive and responsive mission areas that confront irregular challenges, including those of irregular warfare, the Navy will be faced with increasing demand in a fiscally induced capacity constrained environment. Constrained capacity requires a prioritization of areas requiring persistent presence, to include those regions of current or forecast instability. Also required is an understanding of the risk incurred to mission, and to force, if we do not get that priority correct. We must ensure our Navy remains the finest, best trained, and most ready in the world to sustain key mission areas that support confronting irregular challenges, and has the ability to face a highly capable adversary. The Navy looks forward to working with Congress to address our future challenges and thank you for your support of the Navy's mission and personnel at this critical crossroads in U.S. history.[49]

---

[48] At this point, the statement includes a footnote citing the prepared statement of Admiral Jonathan Greenert before the House Armed Services Committee on July 26, 2011. Greenert became the Chief of Naval Operations on September 23, 2011.

[49] Statement of Rear Admiral (Lower Half) Sinclair Harris, Director, Navy Irregular Warfare Office, before the House Armed Services Committee, Subcommittee on Emerging Threats and Capabilities, November 3, 2011. Italics as in original.

# Appendix B. 2012 RAND Corporation Report Findings and Recommendations

This appendix presents findings and recommendations from a 2012 report on maritime regular warfare by RAND Corporation, a research firm.

## Findings

The report made the following findings, among others:

> The study's main findings span the strategic, operational, and tactical levels. Several are specific to MIW, while others have implications both for MIW [maritime irregular warfare] and for IW operations more broadly.
>
> First, *the maritime force is generally considered to play a supportive role to ground forces in IW and therefore has the potential to be underutilized even in IW operations conducted in a predominantly maritime environment....*
>
> Second, *countries that have a prevalent maritime dimension associated with an insurgency could potentially benefit from the enhancement of civil-military operations (CMOs) in the maritime arena....*
>
> Third, *maritime operations in IW can allow the United States to scale its ground involvement in useful ways....*
>
> Fourth, if one assumes that future MIW engagements that entail building a partner's capacity will resemble OEF-P [Operation Enduring Freedom—Philippines], *it is important to manage strategic expectations based on realistic assessments of the partner's capabilities....*
>
> Fifth, *when building partner capacity, either in MIW or land-based IW, the United States should make efforts to provide equipment and technology that the partner will be able to maintain and operate without difficulty....*
>
> Sixth, *with regard to operational methods, coastal maritime interdiction can play an instrumental role in setting the conditions for success in IW by cutting the supply lines that sustain an insurgency....*
>
> Seventh, *as the [1980s] Nicaragua case illustrates, U.S. partners in MIW may only have to influence and monitor the sensibilities of a local population, but the legitimacy of U.S. involvement may be tested in worldwide public opinion....*
>
> Finally, *international cooperation in confronting MIW adversaries is often necessary, and the U.S. Navy should make an effort to ensure that it is tactically and operationally interoperable with partner navies in order to facilitate coordination....* [50]

---

[50] Molly Dunigan, et al, *Characterizing and Exploring the Implications of Maritime Irregular Warfare*, RAND Corporation, Santa Monica (CA), 2012, pp. xv-xviii (italics as in original).

# Recommendations

The report made the following recommendations, among others:

> The findings presented here have several direct implications for the U.S. conventional Navy and Naval Special Warfare Command (NSW). First, U.S. naval forces should continue to provide U.S. partners with suitable equipment that they will be able to operate and maintain and should continually strive to increase their interoperability with partner forces. Second, U.S. naval forces may have to continue or expand training of partner forces to confront future MIW threats. Third, when conducting MIW, operating from a sea base offers advantages to NSW. However, due to the costs of such a practice, both NSW and the conventional Navy must also recognize that decisions regarding when and where to support sea basing of this sort need to be made carefully. Fourth, in support of future MIW operations, NSW is likely to have ongoing requirements for maritime interdiction and containment. Fifth, the United States could benefit from maintaining operational and tactical capabilities with which to assist its partners in surveillance, particularly against small submarines and mining threats. Sixth, NSW should consider increasing its capacity to conduct maritime-based CMOs.
>
> Conventional U.S. naval forces should similarly consider their role in supporting significant irregular ground operations launched from the sea, as well as their role in interdiction and containment campaigns. In contrast to those of NSW, conventional U.S. Navy capabilities to support IW might entail CMOs and related activities to a greater extent than direct action.[51]

---

[51] Molly Dunigan, et al, *Characterizing and Exploring the Implications of Maritime Irregular Warfare*, RAND Corporation, Santa Monica (CA), 2012, pp. xix-xx.

# Appendix C. 2010 Navy Irregular Warfare Vision Statement

This appendix reproduces the Navy's January 2010 vision statement for irregular warfare.[52]

---

[52] Department of the Navy, Chief of Naval Operations, *The U.S. Navy's Vision for Confronting Irregular Challenges*, January 2010, 7 pp. (including the cover page).

# The U.S. Navy's
# Vision for Confronting Irregular Challenges

# January 2010

## CNO Foreword

Our Navy has a history of confronting *irregular challenges* at sea, in the littorals, and on shore. In the face of significant shifts in the nature and character of the threats our nation faces, this Navy Vision for Confronting Irregular Challenges will guide our efforts to prevent, limit, and interdict irregular threats and adversaries. We will focus on the full range of capabilities the Naval force can uniquely project, in and from the maritime domain, in countering *irregular challenges* associated with regional instability, insurgency, crime, and violent extremism.

The *Cooperative Strategy for 21st Century Seapower* places as much emphasis on preventing wars as it does on winning wars, and is the cornerstone of our approach to confronting *irregular challenges*. The six capabilities of our Maritime Strategy, from winning the nation's wars to stabilizing regions with our partners, draws upon the cooperative and preventive capabilities of maritime and joint forces. Our Navy will realize the broadened and balanced capabilities directed in our Maritime Strategy and Defense guidance by making investments to ensure the agility, flexibility, and adaptability necessary to address the range of emergent challenges to our national security. We will enhance integration and interoperability with our traditional maritime partners, the U.S. Marine Corps and U.S. Coast Guard, along with other joint, interagency, private and non-governmental organizations, and international partners in all stages of this effort.

This Vision emphasizes the importance of the maritime contribution to addressing *irregular challenges* in a dynamic and evolving global security environment. The steps we take now will ensure our Navy is prepared fully to work with partners to stabilize regions at risk, and when necessary, dissuade, deter, and defeat irregular actors who seek to undermine security, stability, and prosperity.

G. ROUGHEAD
Admiral, U.S. Navy

2

## I. The Vision for Confronting Irregular Challenges - Pursuing a Capability Balance for 21st Century Operations

<u>**Vision Statement**</u>
*The U.S. Navy will meet irregular challenges through a flexible, agile, and broad array of multi-mission capabilities. We will emphasize Cooperative Security as part of a comprehensive government approach to mitigate the causes of insecurity and instability. We will operate in and from the maritime domain with joint and international partners to enhance regional security and stability, and to dissuade, deter, and when necessary, defeat irregular threats.*

Recognizing the strategic impact of global threats associated with regional instability and insecurity, our Navy has instituted this Vision to guide efforts aimed at confronting *irregular challenges*. In today's interconnected and technically advanced world, **terrorists and criminals prey upon unstable and failing regions and pose an increasing threat to our national interests**. With three-quarters of the world's population, four-fifths of its capital cities, and almost all of its productive capacity located within 200 miles of a coastline, **our Navy is uniquely positioned and suited to counter threats to stability, while operating in and from the maritime domain.** This includes helping countries at risk build sustainable indigenous capacity to secure their resources, protect their populations, and stabilize their regions.

Our Navy must continue efforts to balance emphasis and investments between countering irregular threats and countering near peer forces to successfully meet today's and tomorrow's dynamic and interrelated security challenges. This Vision is derived from our Maritime Strategy and sets a course toward increasing proficiency in supporting direct and indirect approaches to dissuade and defeat *irregular challenges* -- wherein states and non-state actors leverage uncontrolled or ungoverned space to employ informational, economic, technological, and kinetic methods against civilian populations and targets to achieve their objectives. **We will confront *irregular challenges* by focusing on the following outcomes**:

- **Increased effectiveness in stabilizing and strengthening regions**, by securing and leveraging the maritime domain, with and in support of national and international partners.
- **Enhanced regional awareness** of activities and dynamics to include a deeper understanding of ethnic, cultural, and socioeconomic characteristics and norms.
- **Increased regional partner capacity** for maritime security and domain awareness.
- **Expanded coordination and interoperability** with joint, interagency, and international partners.

These outcomes support promoting regional security and stability, advancing the rule of law, promoting good governance and prosperity, and help partners better protect their people and resources. They will inhibit the spread of violent extremism and its associated terrorist, insurgent, and criminal activities.

3

The Navy will leverage its history of presence, international engagement, and security enforcement, and will ensure our sailors, platforms, and systems are ready to address the hybrid nature of 21st Century challenges. The Navy brings global scope, unique access, and a breadth of capabilities to confront *irregular challenges*. We will promote Cooperative Security to mitigate instability in regions with limited governance that give rise to *irregular challenges*. We will enhance proficiency and effectiveness in security force assistance, maritime security, stability operations, information dominance, and other force applications necessary to support U.S. and partner counterinsurgency, counterterrorism, and foreign internal defense operations.

## II. Opportunity: Leveraging the Maritime Domain to Confront Irregular Challenges

*"Covering three-quarters of the planet, the oceans make neighbors of people around the world. They enable us to help friends in need and to confront and defeat aggression far from our shores."*

A Cooperative Strategy for 21<sup>st</sup> Century Seapower

Our Navy's inherent contribution to the irregular contest is our capacity and ability to leverage access to the maritime domain and cooperate with partner navies and security forces to dissuade, deter, and defeat irregular threats at sea and ashore. While often overlooked in the context of *irregular challenges*, **the maritime domain enables proximate populations to partner and enhance their wealth and well-being, but also provides sanctuary and freedom of movement to criminals, terrorists, and insurgents.** The maritime domain provides for over 90% of the flow of information, people, goods, and services that sustain and create opportunities for regional economic prosperity. This economic opportunity promotes stability and helps prevent vulnerable populations from turning to terrorist or criminal enterprises.

The maritime domain similarly provides irregular actors with operating space and the ability to conduct the illicit flow of information, weapons, money, technicians, and cadres upon which much of their income and effectiveness relies. As such they are able to use the maritime environment to exploit, disrupt, or destabilize regions or governments, and to affect the will of civilian populations through insurgency, terrorism, crime, and the proliferation of radical ideologies.

The Navy's global maritime access and sustained presence forward enable U.S. Government-wide partnerships with nations and their forces to provide security and training assistance. At sea and ashore, the Navy works with partners to secure vulnerable maritime approaches and maritime resources, while improving collective capabilities to counter emerging threats such as piracy, trafficking, and weapons proliferation. Partners can appreciate the Navy's dependable but impermanent presence, which requires neither a footprint ashore nor infringement on their sovereignty. Our partners in turn add capability and capacity to our own through their contributions of forces, technologies, and operating concepts, as well as the understanding and ability to navigate local political, ethnic, and cultural contexts.

4

**Today, the Navy is globally engaged to confront *irregular challenges* in sustained joint and interagency operations at sea and ashore.** This includes support for counter-terrorist and counterinsurgency missions, development, humanitarian assistance, disaster response, and maritime security capacity building with partner militaries. Some examples include:

- Support for Joint Special Operations Task Force – Philippines which provides security force training, anti-terrorist forces, and delivered humanitarian relief and disaster response following storm induced flooding.
- Contributions to Joint Task Force – Horn of Africa whose East African Maritime Center of Excellence, security capacity building, and interagency policy efforts are enhancing indigenous capacities to stabilize the region and counter threats of piracy.
- Counter-piracy operations in the Gulf of Aden and the Horn of Africa which remove financial support to terrorists ashore and reduce instability and criminality at sea.
- Training and equipping partners for maritime security and fisheries enforcement in the Gulf of Guinea that many of the region's countries depend for economic stability.
- With coalition partners, the protection of oil platforms in the northern Arabian Gulf, that includes training for Iraqi naval personnel to assume this economically critical mission.
- Expeditionary Training Teams and Global Fleet Stations (Africa, South America, Pacific) dedicated to security force training and assistance through multi-mission employment of amphibious ships, tactical aircraft, and helicopters.
- The over 23,000 Navy personnel engaged in CENTCOM, with 14,000 ashore, conducting maritime security, river patrol, ordnance disposal, surveillance and reconnaissance, electronic warfare, and combat support operations, as well as providing non-naval augmentation for detainee affairs, security, and reconstruction.
- The procurement and employment of evolving multi-mission platforms oriented to lower end operations against *irregular challenges* including: Littoral Combat Ship mission modules, Riverine squadrons tailored for security force assistance, persistent manned and unmanned surveillance platforms, and investments in training capacity for language, cultural, and hybrid mission sets.
- The employment of multi-mission platforms able to work across the spectrum of conflict to include P-3 for surveillance against terrorists and insurgents, tactical aircraft for armed reconnaissance, and submarines and surface combatants in counter-drug operations.

The Navy will continue to pursue balanced approaches to confronting evolving irregular and conventional challenges by maximizing the multi-purpose effectiveness of our Navy's capabilities, personnel, and platforms. We will emphasize building partner capacity using dedicated training forces, periodic deployments and recurring exercises. In the end we will achieve the greatest effectiveness against the most likely 21st Century threats through an agile, flexible, and adaptable force.

5

<u>These goals support the outcomes presented in this Vision:</u>

- **Enhance and formalize interoperability** with U.S. government, public and private organizations, allied maritime and land forces, and regional partners.
- **Build partner capacity** by forming enduring, trust-based relationships, promoting shared interests in collective security, and providing training and resources to enhance indigenous security force capacity.
- **Improve our regional awareness and understanding of complex environments and challenges** through intelligence and information systems, training, education, and more culturally adept approaches.
- **Achieve an improved understanding and ability to counter illicit and extremist actors** as they leverage and maneuver in their maritime and shore environments.
- **Enhance and broaden the multi-mission capabilities and applications of today's force** to maximize effectiveness in complex regions and scenarios.
- **Identify necessary and distinct shifts in emphasis and investment to confront** *irregular challenges*, to include modifications to training, doctrine, and existing forces, and where necessary, new investments in processes, platforms, and systems.

In pursuing these goals for confronting *irregular challenges* the Navy will employ its broad capabilities to enable partners, improve maritime security, and conduct cooperative and decisive operations at sea and ashore. Specifically, we will operate to deny unregulated actors use of the maritime and littoral environment, assist in securing critical infrastructure to ensure the safe flow of resources, and apply a broad spectrum of maritime and overland capabilities to combat irregular threats while improving the lives of affected populations.

## III.  Implementing the Vision

Implementation will require a Navy-wide organizational approach. This effort demands changes in our thinking, our force and its preparation, and requires clear strategic communications within and outside the organization. We will comprehensively align our organizations, investments, procedures, doctrine, and training with the set of emerging approaches necessary to address these challenges.

Our Navy will pursue the outcomes and goals outlined in this Vision through these supporting implementation objectives.

1. **Advance our Navy's doctrinal, strategic, and operational approaches to addressing** *irregular challenges*.
   - Increase our Navy's application of related Defense and Joint strategic and operational guidance.
   - Define the strategic and operational tenets and approaches for our Navy to apply across our general purpose and special operation forces.
   - Integrate the desired outcomes, priorities, and capabilities needed to confront *irregular challenges* into Navy's force development and management processes.

6

2. **Organize, train, and equip our Navy to confront *irregular challenges* more effectively through balancing shifts in our investments and efforts.**
   - Enhance our ability to address, refine, validate, and incorporate urgent and emerging requirements to confront *irregular challenges* in the Planning, Programming, Budgeting, and Execution process.
   - Identify the advocates and resource sponsors responsible for resource allocation and comprehensive program execution for existing and emerging Navy-unique and joint multi-mission capabilities to confront *irregular challenges*.
   - Introduce the necessary supporting training and education requirements, to include organizations, curricula, and processes across our manpower enterprise.
   - Institutionalize concepts, processes, and organizations for training and building the capacity of partners through dedicated assistance operations, regular exercises, and the deployments and visits of multi-mission ships and aircraft.

3. **Emphasize interoperability and effectiveness for confronting *irregular challenges* across U.S. government, public, private, and international partners.**
   - Leverage Navy's multi-mission capabilities with other services, interagency and coalitions to build partner security capacity.
   - Integrate and coordinate efforts with the U.S. Marine Corps and U.S. Coast Guard in support of the imperatives and approaches in the Maritime Strategy.
   - Support the development of joint, interagency, and international operational concepts and supporting CONOPS.
   - Support Defense efforts to integrate joint and interagency planning processes.
   - Ensure capabilities to confront *irregular challenges* are addressed and captured in U.S. Navy and Defense legal policy development.
   - Provide Combatant Commanders with applicable naval capabilities to support critical mission requirements outside the scope of Navy core mission areas.

## IV. Conclusion

Our Navy recognizes the importance of developing opportunities while being prepared to address irregular threats. Our general and special purpose forces are immediately applicable to the broad array of capabilities required to achieve regional security and stability. The Navy is uniquely positioned to assist emerging nations and fragile states, and to dissuade, deter, and when necessary, defeat irregular threats. We will build on our inherent strengths to lead and support national and international efforts.

The *Cooperative Strategy for 21st Century Seapower* places as much emphasis on preventing conflicts as on winning conflicts. This underscores the importance of securing and fostering long-term cooperative relationships based on mutual understanding and respect for each party's strategic interests, as well as increasing partners' ability to ensure their own security and stability. It recognizes the value of presence, of "being there," to maintain adequate levels of security and awareness across the maritime domain, and restrain the destabilizing activities of non-state actors. It makes clear our Navy will work alongside other U.S. services and agencies through a comprehensive government approach to advance international partnerships.

This Vision will guide and shape our Navy's actions, and will enhance our Navy's proficiency in capabilities to counter *irregular challenges*, now and in the future.

7

# Author Contact Information

Ronald O'Rourke
Specialist in Naval Affairs
rorourke@crs.loc.gov, 7-7610

www.ingramcontent.com/pod-product-compliance
Lightning Source LLC
Chambersburg PA
CBHW052022280526
45793CB00005B/1083